# SCHIRMER'S LIBRARY
## OF MUSICAL CLASSICS

### Vol. 1486

# CAMILLE SAINT-SAËNS

# Fourth Concerto
### In C minor
### For the Piano

**Edited by**
**ISIDOR PHILIPP**

# G. SCHIRMER, Inc.

DISTRIBUTED BY

HAL•LEONARD®
CORPORATION
7777 W. BLUEMOUND RD. P.O. BOX 13819 MILWAUKEE, WI 53213

# Fourth Concerto

## I

Edited by
Isidor Philipp

Camille Saint-Saëns. Op. 44

Printed, MCMXLIV, by G. Schirmer, Inc.
Printed in the U. S. A.

4

81967

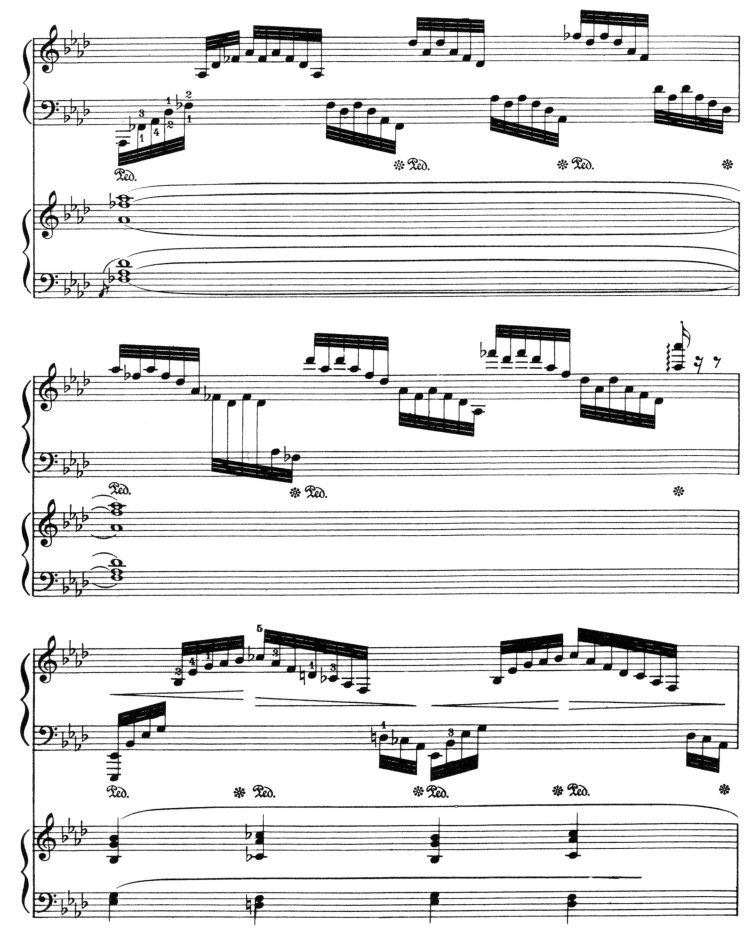

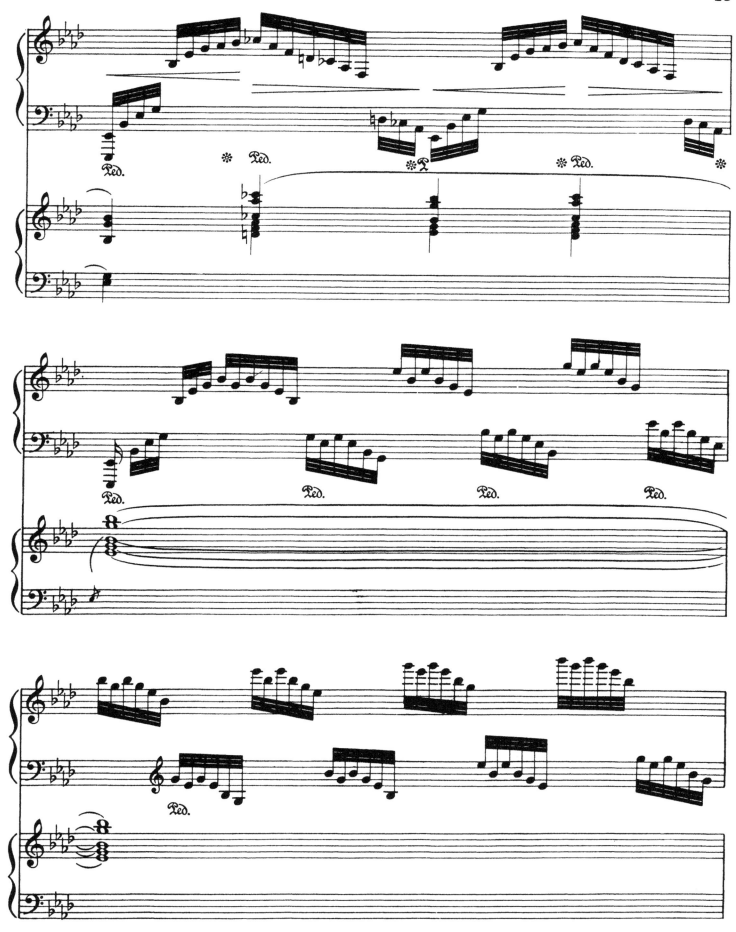

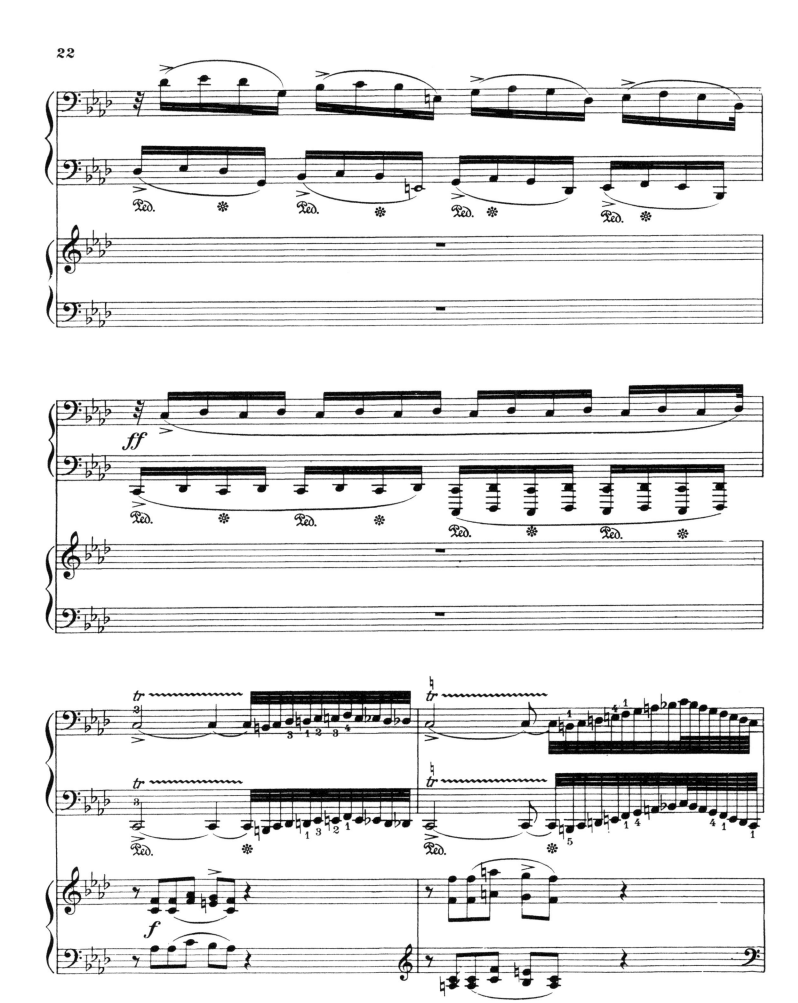

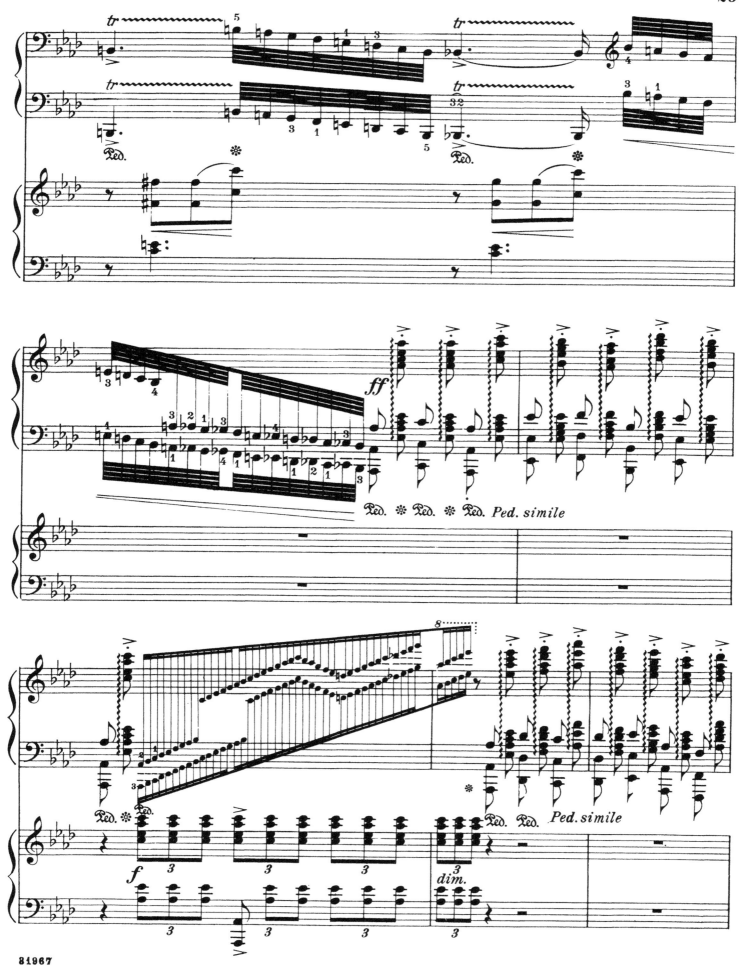

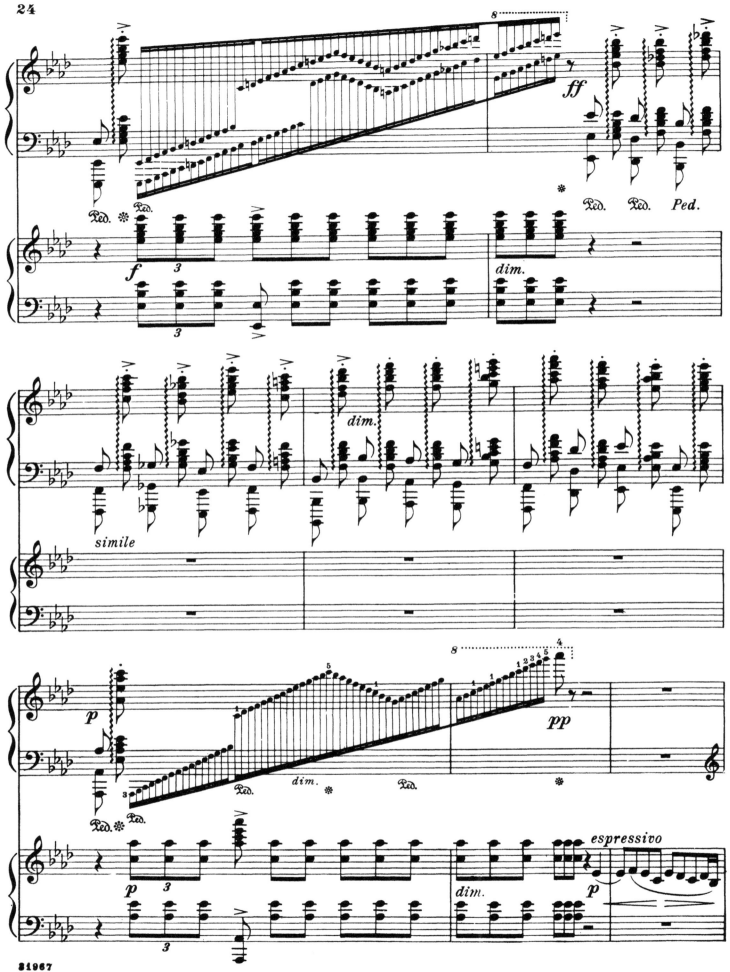

## II

66

31967

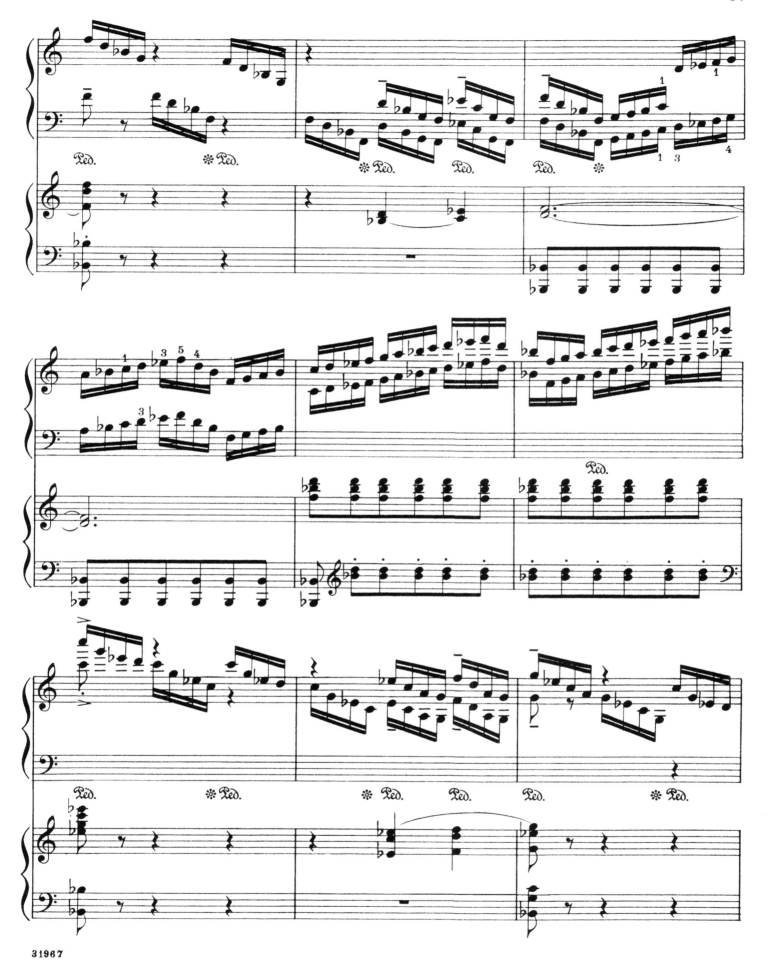

81967